DEDICATION

To my parents, Scott and Linda Doescher and grandparents, Marlin and Iola Doescher and Dennis and Joyce Pempek. Thank you for teaching me that you can accomplish anything with enough hard work and giving me the confidence to go out and do it.

TABLE OF CONTENTS

GOAL OF THIS BOOK

What would you say if I told you that you could improve your family's interactions with each other in just 10 minutes per week? This book will help you do just that!

Now, this book is not meant to be a family savior or solve all problems. Rather, it is meant to make life at home just a little easier, a little *more calm*, and a little more enjoyable. That being said, a little bit of a difference can go a long way. **A tiny change may have a large impact.**

Why is that? Sometimes we don't need things to be a lot easier. We just need them to be a little bit easier. **With our families we just need things to go a little bit better for it to seem a lot better at home.**

DIRECTIONS How To Use This Book

Parents please read the lesson ahead of time and look over the worksheets. Each lesson is meant to be used for 1-2 weeks. Please plan a meeting time of about 10-15 minutes to sit down with the family. Read the script ahead of time and during the meeting please read only the italicized words to the family. PLEASE bring a VERY desirable treat to each meeting and change it up frequently. This is done so that even if the 10 minute meeting is very boring at least we got a good snack out of it! It also can help with grabbing the attention of the kids and helping them engage with the lesson.

Also, although the lessons are numbered they can be done in almost any order. However, I recommend starting with the calendar chapters so that there are tools for organizing and framing activities that can be used with the other lessons.

Helpful PARENT ONLY chapters are found in the back of the book along with pre and post evaluation materials. These should be used prior to starting the lessons and after completion of all lessons to show how families have made progress!

A note on rewards: rewards are meant to grab a kid's attention and help them engage in the meetings and the lessons of the week. The more kids are engaged in the assigned lessons of the week, the more progress a family can expect to make (and the more fun all will have during the process!).

Pre and Post Evaluation materials are provided in Chapter 23. I recommend completing the Pre/Post Evaluation worksheets prior to starting the lessons and upon completion of the lessons.

For helpful video clips and to provide feedback on the *10 Minute Family Solution* please go to *www. hurdpsychology.com.*

Needed: Desirable food or snack. This is just like a work meeting that is improved when someone brings in the "good donuts." Believe it or not this is a critical component.

Needed: 10 minutes only. Set the timer and do not go over. Meetings over 10 minutes are looked at as a drag and they are hard to fit in the schedule.

Needed: Parents should use only positives during the meeting. Say, "We have some great things to try" so that things at home are more content and happy, and they include some good rewards!

Sample Family Meeting Agenda

8:00 Get out the donuts.

8:01 Sit at table, take a bite of a donut, and smile.

8:03 Get out the lesson script for the week and read it.

8:05 Complete the worksheet for the lesson.

8:09 Plan when the next meeting is.

8:10 Adjourn the meeting with a positive comment like, "I really like meeting with you," or "You guys are great!"

One easy and fun way to help kids feel more in control of their lives is to give them their own calendar. This is even helpful for little kids who cannot read yet, as you can draw pictures or put stickers on to show what they will be doing on certain days. The function of the calendar is to show what kids will be doing and when. This helps them to know what is going on in their lives, and what they can expect to happen next.

My adult example of this is: I used to be somewhat of a runner. One time I went on a run with someone who was deciding where we were running and how long. I was almost in a panic just because of the uncertainty regarding the activity. I did not know how long I was going to have to endure this. I did not know where I was going or when it would end. I was out of breath and panicked.

This is what I think happens to kids in life when they think they know what is going on and then there is a change. For example, as school gets out a kid might be thinking, "great, I can go home and play for a while." However, their sibling has a doctor appointment and they are going to have to go along to that instead. This unexpected event can contribute to an upset and some stress. An easy way to prevent this surprise and trouble is to put the appointment on the calendar and plan to bring something really fun along (video game system) or plan to do homework in the waiting room, with the plan to get a treat on the way home if all goes well.

The child should pick out the calendar. A couple of times per week mom/dad and the child can put events on it. Then in the morning and at night the calendar can be consulted to examine upcoming events. It should be a fun activity, and the calendar should always have something fun planned and placed on it, even if the fun event is a few weeks away. This helps to plan something rewarding even if there are a couple of busy weeks planned. It also helps to remind us to sneak some fun into a busy week (like a quick stop for ice cream or a quick stop at the park). It can be a mental organizer, planner, and a tool to create calm and fun.

Directions: Read all ITALICIZED TEXT. Do not read text that is not italicized.

Script for Lesson 1: Calendars (Items needed: 1 printed calendar for each family member, 1 pen for each family member, and markers). PLEASE STICK TO THE SCRIPTS AS MUCH AS YOU CAN!

Parent/Caregiver: *Hello everyone! You all look great today! Would any of you care for a delicious snack? (Pause for effect.) We are going to be having 10 minute weekly family meetings in order to help our home life to be more calm and less stressful. We will be having special snacks during these meetings and will be working towards earning weekly prizes for a job well done over the week.*

Parent/Caregiver: *Today, we are going to start using the organizational tool of a calendar. Calendars help us organize our thoughts and plan for the events in the weeks to come. It helps us know what to expect.*

Parent/Caregiver: *We will all get our own calendars, put a few events on them, and place them on each of our doors. We will try to be detailed with our planning, so we should add things like Doctors appointments and even stopping by Target to pick up a few things. This should help us know what is coming next and help our worlds stay calmer.*

Parent/Caregiver: *We will be using our calendars this week with the hope that we all place some items on the calendar and examine the calendars daily. We will all be working towards earning [a prize like going out for ice cream] at the end of the week.*

Parent/Caregiver: *I would also like for each of us to make sure we carve out a little time for something we like to do this week. We need to make sure we have some fun amidst our busy week!*

Parent/Caregiver: *I have printed off monthly calendars for each of us. Let's put some of our events on the calendars (sports, clubs, or appointments).*

Parent/Caregiver: *Are there any questions? Great job all!!!!*

Prize bank Ideas: Pizza night, movie night, or ice cream sundae night. What are other ideas you can think of?

_____'s Calendar   Month _____

SUNDAY	MONDAY	TUESDAY	WEDNESDAY	THURSDAY	FRIDAY	SATURDAY

Directions: place all items on _____'s calendar and visit the calendar daily.

Well, it is that time of year again. It is time for holiday cheer and the sweetness of this time of year. It is simultaneously the time of year for present buying, wrapping, delivering, spending, cooking, making (buying supplies, making them, delivering them), planning, going, visiting, doing and go and go and go and go.

Wow, as much fun as that sounds, I feel chaotic and tired just writing this. So for kids that have trouble in a classroom full of noise and children, it is easy to see why they might struggle with the holiday chaos. While the thoughts of Christmas and holiday cheer make them smile, in actuality the lack of routine and unexpected activities, combined with excitement tends to overload many of them to the breaking point. I thought that this was supposed to be fun! I bought these things for you and I am doing all these things for you. Why are you not having fun!!!!????!!!!

My main recommendation would be "quality over quantity." While it seems fun to do lots and lots of holiday events, birthday activities, and other special events, cutting down on the number may be beneficial to all involved.

This all applies to vacations as well. We often would like to cram as much as we can into a vacation so that we maximize the experience. However, if too many vacation activities lead to upsets then the vacation is not nearly as fun for all. So doing a little less so that the group remains happier can go a long way to increasing the overall enjoyment of the vacation. The planning tools provided can give some structure to vacations that can bring a sense of calm (and enhance the fun!).

Directions: Read all ITALICIZED TEXT. Do not read text that is not italicized.

Script for Lesson 2: Holidays, Vacation, and Chaos (Items needed: 1 printed weekly calendar for each family member, and 1 pen/marker for each family member). PLEASE STICK TO THE SCRIPTS AS MUCH AS YOU CAN!

Parent/Caregiver: *Hi guys! Wonderful to see all of you! Would any of you care for a delicious snack?* (Pause for effect.)

Parent/Caregiver: *Today we are going to plan to have a great holiday/vacation season by doing some careful planning and making sure we take enough down time for each of us. Holidays/Vacations can be really fun but they can also be busy and tiring! We want to make sure that the holiday seasons are as fun as they are intended to be!*

Parent/Caregiver: *We will all get our own [holiday/vacation] calendars, put a few events on them, and place them on each of our doors. These calendars should have some holiday events on them like shopping, wrapping, making cookies, getting the tree, etc. The calendars should also have at least a 15 minute down time break scheduled for each family member at home in order to do some "chilltime." This is very important for many people in order to feel more calm and happy.*

Parent/Caregiver: *We will be using our calendars this week with the hope that we all place some items on the calendar and examine the calendars daily. We will all be working towards earning [something from your prize bank] at the end of the week.*

Parent/Caregiver: *I have printed off holiday calendars for each of us. Let's put some of our holiday events on the calendars.*

Parent/Caregiver: *Are there any questions? Wonderful work all!!!!*

Prize Bank Ideas: Pizza night, movie night, ice cream sundae night, special holiday idea like picking out a new ornament. Can you think of other prize ideas?

HOLIDAY OR VACATION CALENDAR
What to expect and fun planning calendar

SUNDAY	MONDAY	TUESDAY	WEDNESDAY	THURSDAY	FRIDAY	SATURDAY

Plan quiet break time daily.

2.2 Holiday Schedule Worksheet

When it comes to giving kids choices: less is more.

One idea we sometimes have for making kids happy would be to let them choose things (things to eat, things to do, fun things, etc). However, in reality giving kids too many choices, or sometimes choices at all can be a backfiring disaster. Case in point: a family goes to Disney world and they ask the child, which ride would you like to go on first? Where would you like to eat? What would you like to order? What souvenir would you like? Wow, my head is spinning with these questions and the plethora of possibilities. Oh, the pressure. It can make kids heads spin too, and when that happens kids start to feel uneasy. Choices and planning largely should be the role of the adult, because while it seems fun, it can add stress to a child for them to make decisions.

Now, of course if the child wants to ride the tea cups then of course he should be able to ride them at Disney World. However, this is where "making a plan" comes in (see Worksheet 3.3). Because what if we say OK Johnny what ride do you want to start with? He says the teacups. Then we realize the tea cups are 20 minutes from where we are standing. So we try to alter the plan and tell Johnny that we are going to start on Space Mountain because it is closer. Johnny has a huge meltdown right there in the land of happiness. Headaches ensue with parents thinking all I did was take him to Disney World and this is the thanks I get.

So in making a general plan ahead of time using the park map found online you can draw up a tentative plan with input from each kiddo. However, now we have a visual idea of what the day might look like. Everyone in the family should have one item for the "must-do" activity at Disney World. That way each person was able to make a choice. Thinking ahead of time what the schedule might look like is actually helpful to all people. To make kids feel even better about it, go online and look for some photos of what walking around at Disney World would look like. Another benefit of the tentative schedule, is that if a conflict comes up with two people wanting differing ideas, just say "Well, I better pull out the schedule and get these things on there!"— What great ideas. It gives a tool for navigating possible conflicts and a way to plan to get things accomplished.

These organizational tools can also be used with much benefit on weekends or other days off from school. Either the night before or the morning of sit with each child for 5 minutes and draw up "the plan for the day." The structured choice sheet can be used any day in order to help children give input but in a structured way. These tools will help to organize and calm the thoughts of children and over time can help reduce the amount of upsets throughout our weeks. For example, instead of saying "we are going to the store after school" which we know will lead to an argument we could say to the child, "would you like to go to "Kmart or Target?" Instead of "get in the car" try "would you like to get in the right or the left side of the car?" I know — it sounds looney. There are reasons why this tool is helpful so if you would like additional information go to the blog website for a short video with helpful hints from me. Otherwise give using these tools a try and see if they don't improve the level of the arguing. (The kids will still complain it just might not be a yelling fit or at the high level of frustration).

Directions: Read all ITALICIZED TEXT. Do not read text that is not italicized.

PLAN THIS MEETING ON A WEEKEND DAY SO YOU CAN TRY OUT THE DAILY SCHEDULE.

Script for Lesson 3: Give Structure (Items needed: grab the calendars from the doors for each family member, 1 pen for each family member, and markers). PLEASE STICK TO THE SCRIPTS AS MUCH AS YOU CAN!

Parent/Caregiver: *Hi all! Great to see you all for a bit today! Would any of you care for a little snack (make sure to change it up!)?* (Pause for effect.)

Parent/Caregiver: *Today we are going to discuss planning some of our unstructured days such as weekends, days off, or vacation days.*

Parent/Caregiver: *When we plan out a vacation or weekend day it can make the day go more smoothly!*

Parent/Caregiver: *We are going to spend the next few minutes planning out the rest of today. We will list all items including running errands, free time, chores, dinner, playing with friends, etc. Let's make sure we include at least one thing each of us considers fun!*

Parent/Caregiver: *We should note that this is a rough plan of the day and we may need to add something or make a change. For example, we might realize we forgot an ingredient to make dinner so we may have to run out to pick it up! If that happens we may add that item to the daily schedule.*

Parent/Caregiver: *Are there any questions? This is probably an easy one!!!!*

Choice Sheet

Directions: please place two choices below for a child to select in order to gain some child input, but also provide structure in the day's events. You can write the choices or draw them for a young child. The child can circle his or her choice.

OR

Choose answer

Daily Plan EXAMPLE for Vacation Date _____

1. Get up

2. Eat breakfast and get ready at the hotel

3. Leave for Disney

4. Start on the trolley and get in line

5. Go inside and head for the castle

6. Tea cups ride?

7. Take a break for lunch
   a. Reapply sunscreen

8. Mine rides

9. How did I do?
   a. Video games for ride home
   b. Were there rides to put on our list for tomorrow?

Bring a pen. There may have to be changes if there is a long line or it starts raining.

The Plan for Today: _____(list date)

1.

2.

3.

4.

5.

6.

7.

8.

9.

10.

11.

12.

13.

14.

15.

Bring a pen. There may have to be changes if there is a long line or it starts raining.

What if the schedule has to change? Plan when you can schedule what was missed and put it on the calendar!

This may be the most powerful interventions of all time when it comes to kids.

Simply put, give 10 minutes of your time solely to each of your children per weekday. The caveat of this is no TV, no radio, no computer, no tablet, and no electronics. Also, no daydreaming or thinking of what else you need to be doing. (In this society, this part may be the hardest, as our minds naturally drift towards work, dinner, chores, and other things we "should" be doing).

One important thing: do not ask the child what he or she wants to do with you. Sit down with the child and together make a list of 20 games, toys, activities or things that you could do together. Either write a list of these activities or draw out these activities. Then refer to the sheet on a daily basis if ideas are needed.

Second important thing: Smile. Be goofy. Be silly. Laugh. If you need a jump start, think of a few things you two really enjoy together... going for ice cream, going to the park, going skating, making a favorite recipe.... and start there. Or start with a very preferred activity of the child.

Third important thing: doing things separately with the kids give each of them individual attention and also gives you unique connections with each child. There is a different dynamic for some kids when they are one on one with you, rather than vying for your attention.

I dare you to try this for one month. I would love to hear the results. They can be life changing.

Directions: Read all ITALICIZED TEXT. Do not read text that is not italicized.

Script for Lesson 4: 10 Minutes of Undivided Attention (Items needed: grab the calendars from the doors for each family member, 1 pen for each family member, and markers). PLEASE STICK TO THE SCRIPTS AS MUCH AS YOU CAN!

Parent/Caregiver: *Hi all! Wow, you look fabulous today! Would any of you care for a delicious snack (make sure to change it up!)? (Pause for effect.)*

Parent/Caregiver: *Today we are going to make sure that we spend 10 minutes per week of time doing something we like to do together.*

Parent/Caregiver: *Life gets busy but I really enjoy doing many, many things with each of you. Sometimes our weeks get so busy that we do not have time for those things, but that is going to change!*

Parent/Caregiver: *We are going to spend the next few minutes of brainstorming things for you to do 1:1 with me (and _____). (Hand out brainstorming sheets) This could be playing a game or horsing around outside, things you like to do together.*

Parent/Caregiver: *One of the challenges is that during a busy weeks we may not have time for these things, so we will make time by planning ahead and putting them on our calendar.*

Parent/Caregiver: *We will be placing one item on our calendar to do one on one with mom/dad/caregiver. Let's put the items on the calendars! We will all be working towards earning [something like a special trip to mini golf] at the end of the week if we complete this mission.*

Parent/Caregiver: *Are there any questions? This is the easiest one yet!!!!*

Prize Bank Ideas: *Mini golf outing, Frisbee golf outing, or playing around outside at favorite park. Can you think of other ideas?*

The Plan

Play **10** minutes of _____ together with kids and parent/s (examples include: preferred activity, cool activity like soccer, baseball, basketball, game, Legos)

Set timer and then get special cookies or ice cream or tell a new joke (or some other fun way to end).

End on a high note!

If it was fun, put it on the schedule for tomorrow!

Yay!!!!!

The Plan: 10 Minutes Daily

Playing: game of choice, toy, outside time, or other ideas:_____

Rule: no devices such as cell phones/TV/tablet/computer

Did we do it every day?

MONDAY	TUESDAY	WEDNESDAY	THURSDAY	FRIDAY	SATURDAY	SUNDAY

Great! If we remembered we all get _____! Yay!

Many families with children who have worked with me know what I refer to as "silly voice week" where we only speak to each other in silly voices or as different make-believe characters.

If only I had a nickel for every time I heard a kid tell me that one of his parents "yells" at him all the time. When investigating the incident there is no actual raising of the voice volume. However it is likely that we all know what someone means when they say so and so was "yelling" at me. They mean that the voice did not sound very nice.

A voice that sounds stressed, impatient, frustrated, annoyed, or disappointed. These voices can pierce a child and hurt them deeply — it does not matter how they speak back. (Of course it is not OK with children to speak disrespectfully). However, we have to rise above and speak to children with calm, loving voice.

Children and all of us are creatures of habit. So one fun way to break up this habit is silly voice week. It can be fun too, if you own it. It can also be a barometer of how silly you are on a regular basis. If this is a hard task, then it is incredibly important you take steps toward doing this! Children need fun and silly! Give it a shot.

I would love to hear from you. Did this assignment increase laughter at your house????

LESSON 5.1: Be Silly

Directions: Read all ITALICIZED TEXT. Do not read text that is not italicized.

Script for Lesson 4: Be Silly (Items needed: print the sheet for the week, and markers). PLEASE STICK TO THE SCRIPTS AS MUCH AS YOU CAN!

Parent/Caregiver: *Hi family! You are such a nice group to meet with! Would any of you care for a delicious snack (make sure to change it up!)? (Pause for effect.)*

Parent/Caregiver: *Today we are going to bring a bit of silliness back to the family at home.*

Parent/Caregiver: *Sometimes life gets so busy and serious that the fun just goes down down down. We also tend to get frustrated with each other and can talk with a not nice tone to each other. We are all culprits for this.*

Parent/Caregiver: *This week we are going to do our best to bring back a little fun and silliness to the family by talking in goofy or accented voices for the week. This should be silly and also should break it up if accidentally we have been talking in a less than nice and respectful manner to each other.*

Parent/Caregiver: *We will be using our mission sheet to brainstorm silly voices such as Alien, Squirrel voice, or Darth Vader.*

Parent/Caregiver: *We will choose a silly voice or action for each day of the week and put up the plan in the kitchen. We will all be working towards earning [something like go to the movies] at the end of the week if we complete this mission.*

Parent/Caregiver: *Are there any questions? I dare you to stay serious and try not to laugh this week!!!!*

Prize Bank Ideas: *Match prize with the voice such as get the Star Wars Movies if you chose Darth Vader voice.*

The Plan: Pick a Goofy Voice/Action!

Ideas: Princess/Royalty voice, old woman voice, alien voice, computer voice, English accent, or Pig Latin.

Other Silly Ideas: Skip everywhere, walk backwards, wear a goofy hat, or choose something else!

What did we decide on?_____

MONDAY	TUESDAY	WEDNESDAY	THURSDAY	FRIDAY	SATURDAY	SUNDAY

Did try to do it? Yeah! We earn _____

Ideas include: pizza or movie night.

Was there more laughter at our house? _____

Kids can do more than we think they can. They watch us like hawks since early on and they want to be just like you. So one way to get more connected is to arrange for a small activity where they can do what you are doing. Invite your child to join you in a task and give them a child-safe version to do themselves. This will bring you closer and make the child feel important.

One example of this, was I had the pleasure of hanging out with two sweet, smart 2½ year olds a month back. I was baking cookies and as it turns out, they were interested. So as I baked my own cookies, I set them each on a chair pushed up to a table and gave them bowls with some baking materials (spoons, measuring cups). Each time I added an ingredient to my bowl, I also added one to each of theirs (of course I did not give them eggs or anything that could potentially be problematic). I decided beforehand that this had the potential to be messy and I was OK with that. I added flour first and they delighted in mixing, measuring, and feeling it. And I talked about my baking process with them in a fun, childlike way.

I had no idea that "Baking 101" with 2 year olds could be such a hit. When I added sugars, I would also add a small amount to theirs and then encourage them to "mix it in so we could make delicious cookies." I was astounded at how well they did with this. I was even tempted to try baking theirs just to see what would happen because they did so well (I came to my senses and did not). Their interest was held exceptionally long and they were very engaged in the process with me. They obviously had fun and I think because there was an element of genuine baking, and it resonated even with little ones.

Directions: Read all ITALICIZED TEXT. Do not read text that is not italicized.

Script for Lesson 6: Let Them Do Their Own Projects with Your Materials (Items needed: print the sheet for the week, get our calendars from our doors, and markers). PLEASE STICK TO THE SCRIPTS AS MUCH AS YOU CAN!

Parent/Caregiver: *Hi group! You are marvelous family members! Would any of you care for a delicious snack (make sure to change it up!)?* (Pause for effect.)

Parent/Caregiver: *Today we are going to plan to do some special, grown up projects together.*

Parent/Caregiver: *Sometimes life gets so busy we get used to hearing, "no," and this time it is going to be "yes."*

Parent/Caregiver: *This week we are going to brainstorm some grown up projects like baking, creating, building or doing. We are going to start to complete one together.*

Parent/Caregiver: *We will be using our mission sheet to brainstorm ideas to do together such as bake red velvet cupcakes or build a model ship or car. Let's get out our brainstorming sheet now. What ideas can we come up with? We could even use the Internet to search how to do something.*

Parent/Caregiver: *We will choose a project to complete with each parent and place a time for working on this on our calendars.*

Parent/Caregiver: *Are there any questions? This may be easy to complete or may take some time. We may have to do several prototypes in order to be successful!!!!*

Things to make will be the prizes of the week unless the project was a flop, then A for effort and pick an alternative prize for the week!

The Plan: Create a project for kids to help with or do their own interest.

Ideas: Bake or cook an item of the kid's choosing, and take the lead on getting items and making it. (Note: it may not turn out, but it may be fun anyways)

What is the project? _____

_____

Who is doing it? _____

_____

When are we doing it? _____

_____

How much can we spend? _____

What supplies do we need? _____

_____

OK. Game on!

In the dead of winter sometimes it may just be time to try something new. One trick to this idea is to go to the dollar store and pick out some very inexpensive things, either with the child or without. That way it is not costly if this experiment fails.

The act of going and picking out something to do together can be fun in itself. However, if going to stores tends to cause trouble within the family unit then I recommend you going to pick out a few items on your own. Then when it is "special fun day" at home the child can go and pick out a new thing from the "special fun box" for you to explore together.

Sometimes we all need a breath of fresh air. The dollar store trick brings in something new and fun. Another thing to try if you have the opportunity, is going to spend time in different scenery. Perhaps visit a water park for the afternoon or a small overnight hotel getaway with a pool. It is strange how the change in surroundings can break up some of the monotony of this time of year, and also break up some of the interactions with each other in a positive way!

One key to remember when doing something new: sometimes for children trying new things can throw them off. If this is the case, some planning and preparation will need to go into the "be fresh" idea. For instance, use the week to plan the trip to the water park. What does it look like (find pictures online)? What will I do there? How long will we stay? What might we eat there?

Another trick to success is less choices for children. Avoid questions like do you want to do _____? Which one would you like to choose? Believe it or not, sometimes choices can be anxiety provoking and lead to arguing. I recommend planning out beforehand some of these things so that there is a basic plan, and not too much in the moment choices for kids.

LESSON 7.1: Be Fresh

Directions: Read all ITALICIZED TEXT. Do not read text that is not italicized.

Script for Lesson 7: Be Fresh (Items needed: print the sheet for the week, get our calendars from our doors, and markers). PLEASE STICK TO THE SCRIPTS AS MUCH AS YOU CAN!

Parent/Caregiver: *Hi All! Great job on these missions, you guys rock! Would any of you care for a delicious snack (make sure to change it up!)?* (Pause for effect.)

Parent/Caregiver: *Today we are going to get some new, fresh ideas for activities going.*

Parent/Caregiver: *Sometimes, especially in the Winter months, things start to feel a bit stale or boring. We need to liven things up a bit with some new ideas.*

Parent/Caregiver: *This week we are going to brainstorm some fresh ideas to do this Winter to keep us from getting cabin fever and getting cranky.*

Parent/Caregiver: *We will be using our mission sheet to brainstorm ideas to do such as go to hear some music together, check out a play, or sledding/skating/skiing. Let's get out our brainstorming sheet now. What ideas can we come up with? We could use the Internet to search how to do something (or local paper or City Pages).*

Parent/Caregiver: *What were the best ideas we came up with? Let's try to get one a week on our calendars at least.*

Parent/Caregiver: *Are there any questions? Did we find some hurdles to getting these things accomplished, like being busy? It's OK to plan things a few weeks in advance if that's what needs to happen to get it on the calendar!!!*

Ideas to make things more fun and exciting during the winter months

Dollar Store, Goodwill $5 Adventure

Head to the warmth, small water park (look for coupons)

Family date night (dinner and movie)

Winter festivals (look in local pages)

Local bands or plays

Kid ideas:

(Ice skating, sledding, skiing, etc.)

Start putting these on the calendar!

Ideas Sheet Worksheet 7.2

So this is an idea for a lesson that I need more help putting into practice myself. However, I will give you the tidbits that actually work for me....

1. Less is more: the less out and about that you can see, the more internally calm people tend to feel. Case in point: how do you feel in a kindergarten classroom that has 5 different artworks by 25 students on the wall. Above that is the alphabet and number line. On another wall is school mottoes, posters, in every bright color imaginable......

2. To declutter, try doing this once per week. Get some decorative boxes from Michaels or JoAnns and put clutter into the boxes (ideally sort the clutter, but perhaps just boxing things up at first).

3. Simplify everyday items. For example, run the dishwasher at the same time everyday (even if it is not completely full). This helps make sure dishes are clean and also prevents the problem of the dishwasher getting full and dirty dishes piling up on the counter.

4. Problem Solve — how could I have avoided this problem? What could make this easier to get this done?

5. Automate — CELL PHONE reminders!!!!!! Daily alarms to remind us of things during the day/week/month and day before reminders for important things

When we are more organized we feel less anxious! Less clutter equals a feeling of calm and order. This setting will help us feel less overwhelmed by life and provide some tranquility in our homes. A little bit of organizing can go a long way!

Directions: Read all ITALICIZED TEXT. Do not read text that is not italicized.

Script for Lesson 8: Be Organized (Item needed: print the sheets for the week). PLEASE STICK TO THE SCRIPTS AS MUCH AS YOU CAN!

Parent/Caregiver: *Hello good-looking family! Nice to see you today! Would any of you care for a yummy snack (make sure to change it up!)?* (Pause for effect.)

Parent/Caregiver: *Today we are going to talk about organization.*

Parent/Caregiver: *When our home and rooms that we spend time in are neat and organized, it can help us to feel more calm within ourselves.*

Parent/Caregiver: *Sometimes cleaning and organizing can feel overwhelming. However if we start with one or two small tasks at a time, we can make a big difference in how we feel at home.*

Parent/Caregiver: *Here is a sheet that gives examples of some ideas for organizing our rooms and the events in our lives. How could our rooms be more organized? Do we need some additional items to make organization and cleaning easier?* (Such as bins, containers, labels, etc.)

Parent/Caregiver: *What are some easy ways to pick up clutter and keep it clean?*

Parent/Caregiver: *How would the space feel with the addition of something like a new paint color, a soft lamp, soft music playing, a non cluttered/cleaned up space?*

Parent/Caregiver: *Great job!* (No matter what they said)

Parent/Caregiver: *What is one thing we can each do to organize better this week? Let's put it on the calendar so we know we have made time for this. What can our prize be for the week? Some ideas could include working towards some room redecorating (like wall color, bed spread, rug, lamp, or soft music).*

What things would help home to feel happier and calmer?

Brainstorm: _____

_____

_____

_____

_____

_____

_____

_____

_____

Ideas:
+ Can we organize better?
+ Is there something we always lose? Can we make a special place for that?
+ Is there something that would make our spaces calmer? Soft music?
+ Something additional for our rooms? Soft lighting/lamp?
  Making 10 min for something happy and calm each day.

Which ones will we try?: _____

_____

_____

_____

_____

_____

_____

_____

Goal of the week for the family:

Example:
Put away what we take out
Place dishes in dishwasher
Start it up nightly and empty in AM

How did we do?

MONDAY	TUESDAY	WEDNESDAY	THURSDAY	FRIDAY	SATURDAY	SUNDAY

Earn:

(Example: A trip to waterpark! Yes!!!)

Did we struggle on a certain day? What can we do about it?

8.3 Calmer Home Plan Worksheet 2

This is a critical lesson. If something happens at school in which the child gets "in trouble" then almost certainly the kiddo already feels bad enough. It is also most likely that they already received some sort of expected punishment. It is very important that the child is NOT punished at home for a mistake that was already punished at school.

Certainly there can be a discussion of what could go differently next time using the problem-solving model on the next page. In using the problem-solving model we take the blame out of the equation and instead discuss what are other options and their consequences or outcomes. We draw them out (options and consequences of actions) and then let the child discuss and pick the choice that is actually the best one. These exercises can be telling in that sometimes in the moment children have a hard time figuring out that there is more than one option available.

The message at home should be no matter what happens at school or anywhere, at home you are loved and we will just try our best tomorrow. I also consider the home to be the "sanctuary" of happy and calm. The chaos of life can continue on outside of the house, but the house should be set up to encourage family calm, fun, and love. It should set all parties up to be successful when they step out of the house. Sometimes a small change can go a very long way in making people feel more calm and grounded.

Directions: Read all ITALICIZED TEXT. Do not read text that is not italicized.

Script for Lesson 9: Problem Solving (Items needed: print the sheets for the week). PLEASE STICK TO THE SCRIPTS AS MUCH AS YOU CAN!

Parent/Caregiver: *Good (morning/afternoon/evening) group! You are all amazing in your own way! Would any of you care for a yummy snack (make sure to change it up!)?* (Pause for effect.)

Parent/Caregiver: *Today we are going to talk about problem solving.*

Parent/Caregiver: *Throughout our days we each encounter various problems (ranging from small to big). How we deal with those problems can make a big difference in how we feel the rest of the day.*

Parent/Caregiver: *None of us are perfect. All of us have problems that we encounter and mistakes that we make (grownups and kids!).*

Parent/Caregiver: *However, if a mistake is made at school it is ok, we will work on making sure it does not happen again. And no matter what happened, you are loved no matter what.*

Parent/Caregiver: *If we have to talk about some problem solving or things to improve we will schedule a little "meeting" on our calendars (15 minutes or less). That way, we only focus a little bit on this at home, and the rest of the time we can focus on family and positives.*

Parent/Caregiver: *Here is a sheet to guide problem solving. It involves identifying the problem. It then allows for listing 4 different choices as to how to handle the problem, and a consequence of each choice. Then at the bottom we can select the best choice.*

Parent/Caregiver: *We might use the problem solving sheet to solve a made-up problem, or we might examine a problem that one of us encountered during our scheduled meeting. This allows for discussing how to think about our options and how to make a better choice next time.*

Parent/Caregiver: *Great job!* (No matter what they said.)

Parent/Caregiver: *Let's schedule one small problem-solving meeting on our calendars this week. One for each child individually. Did we meet and talk about solving problems? What can we earn this week as a reward? Special dessert or snack to pick up perhaps?*

Problem Solving

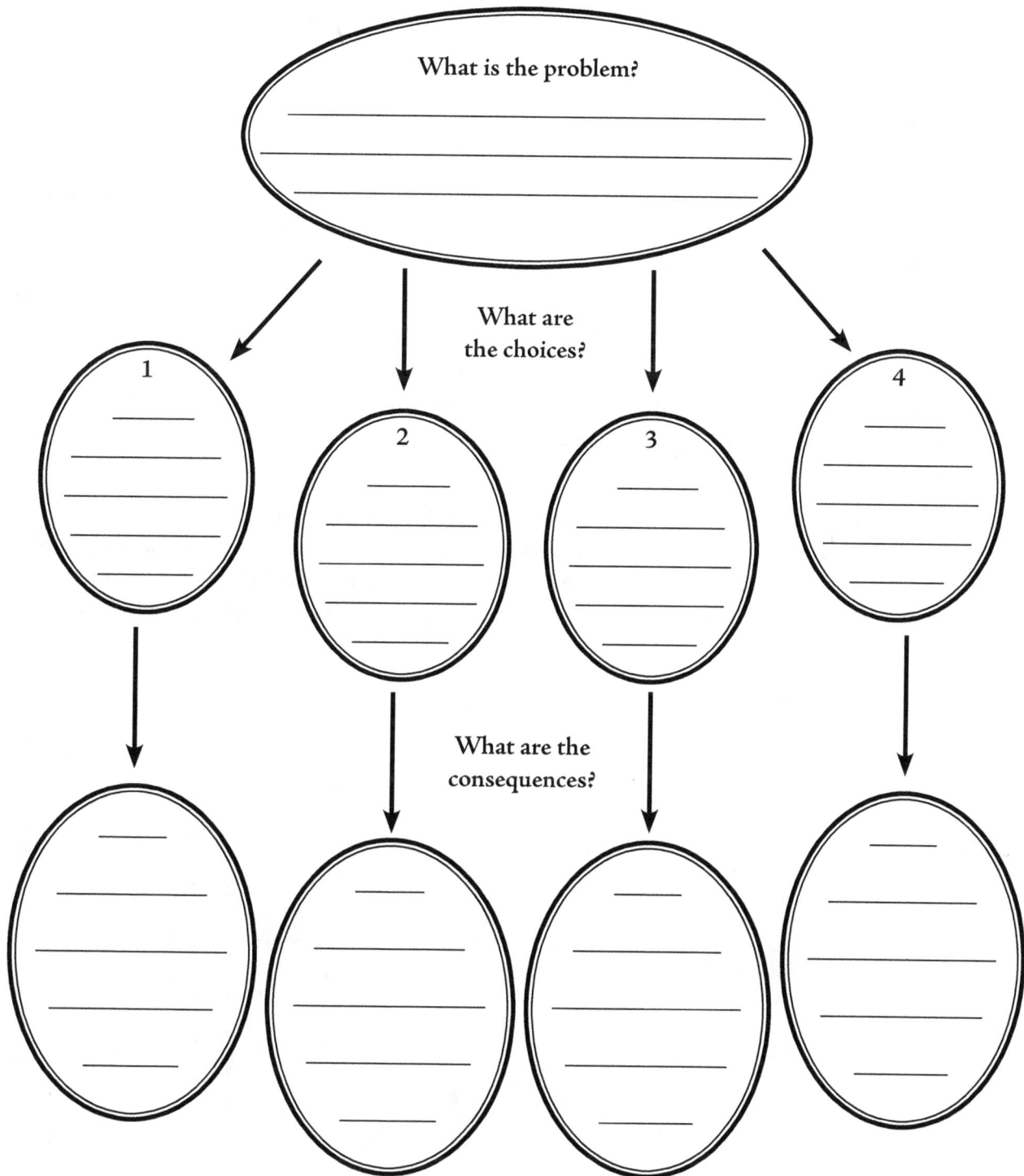

What is the problem?

_____

_____

_____

What are
the choices?

1

___

___

___

___

2

___

___

___

___

3

___

___

___

4

___

___

___

What are the
consequences?

Which is the best choice? # _____ **Why?** _____

"I did absolutely nothing ......
and it was everything I thought it could be."
Office Space

I truly think this is something all of us would benefit from. Definitely.

For some kids this is a necessity. I have seen an influx of kiddos lately that have been so upset by thinking they could go home and chill after school, but instead found out that this was not the plan at all. Instead they had to go to: the store, an appointment, a sibling's appointment, to pick up mom/dad, etc. This led to a large scale, upset of gargantuan proportion and led parents to be baffled. "All we did was stop at the store, but _____ had a tantrum.

Fortunately, I can relate so much to these kids. I relate it to thinking I can be somewhere at 5pm, but then there was a meeting tacked on to the end of the day. Now I have to stay until 7pm, and I have not eaten enough. Plus, I have an early morning the next day. Well this could cause a mini-meltdown for me... so I can relate to the kids.

One way to get around this for kids: First, use the calendar from Lesson 1. Second, use the calendar to schedule 15 minutes of "nothing" per day. That way it is scheduled and the kid can breathe a sigh of relief. In a world in which kids do not control much, they can always count on this small span of time as their own, that no one can touch. A mini-break for the mind. Again, I think all people would benefit from this.

LESSON 10.1: 15 Minutes of Downtime per Day

Directions: Read all ITALICIZED TEXT. Do not read text that is not italicized.

Script for Lesson 10: 15 Minutes of Downtime (Items needed: print the sheet for the week, get our calendars from our doors, and markers). PLEASE STICK TO THE SCRIPTS AS MUCH AS YOU CAN!

Parent/Caregiver: *Hello magnificent family! Nice to meet with all of you! Would any of you care for a scrumptious snack* (make sure to change it up!)? (Pause for effect.)

Parent/Caregiver: *Today we are going to make sure we all get a little bit of a break for ourselves every day!*

Parent/Caregiver: *With our busy schedule sometimes we run out of time to just take "me time" and breathe for a couple of minutes. By giving ourselves a "break" or "reset" it can calm and center us, relieving a bit of stress that naturally builds during the course of a busy day.*

Parent/Caregiver: *Because things can become so busy that we lose this down time — we are going to schedule 15 minutes each day for ourselves to do something quiet that we enjoy doing.*

Parent/Caregiver: *It says here that unfortunately our 15 minutes should not be spent on screentime for a variety of reasons. However, some ideas for this small window of time include: reading, doing crafts or art, Legos, music, building, or a quiet toy.*

Parent/Caregiver: *We will be using our mission sheet to brainstorm ideas for our own downtime (we may already know what each of us would choose. Let's get out our brainstorming sheet now. What ideas can we come up with?*

Parent/Caregiver: *What were the best ideas we came up with? Let's try to schedule our 15 minute downtime on our calendars so that it is a priority in our day.*

Parent/Caregiver: *Are there any questions? Did we find some hurdles to getting these things accomplished, like being busy? It's OK to plan things a few weeks in advance if that's what needs to happen to get it on the calendar!!!*

DO NOT DISTURB

IN

15 MINUTE

RESET

CRITICAL IMPORTANCE!

Reset Space Planning: Need an Absolutely Quiet Area

1. Where was the location decided on? _____

2. What should be there? _____

Ideas include: Art supplies, Legos, headphones or music, quiet play toys, possibly a new special quiet toy, books, or a magazine

Rule: No electronics or screen time

3. PARENT — you do this too!

4. Where was the location decided on? _____

5. What should be there? _____

Set a 15 minute timer! Even 10 minutes will help.

In this busy world there is one question and answer that can help us as we move forward: how do I feel? Research shows that if we can identify how we feel and the reason and can communicate this to others it fosters self regulation. Translation: telling others how we are feeling can lead to being calmer and having more self control. It can also help others understand us better and can lead to other's changing how they react.

Research shows that if we ask for something from another person and give a reason, we are significantly more likely to get what we asked for —and get this, even if it is a bad reason. So, if a child can say to others, "I feel mad because _____," it will help to calm down the child and will also help to calm down those around him/her.

The reason can be dealt with later. At the point that the child is able to communicate his/her feelings, the adult should respond with "I hear you, you feel _____" or "I understand, you feel _____." That way, the child can at the very minimum realize that the other person gets it, they are having a hard time. And if we try really hard, we may be able to relate to them feeling this way.

Second, after figuring out why the child is upset, then we can deal with the reason for their being upset. Sometimes there is no one to blame, but the child is blaming the parent anyway. We all wish there were more hours in the day and that we could make it to dance class, get homework done, and still make it to that restaurant they want to go to. Lack of time is our common enemy — not mom or dad. Explaining this when the child is completely calm is worth a shot.

The Calendar solution: One way to solve many of these issues is to pull out a calendar and plan when we can do the coveted activity. See Lesson #1 for more suggestions on this.

LESSON 11.1: How Do I Feel?

Directions: Read all ITALICIZED TEXT. Do not read text that is not italicized.

Script for Lesson 11: I Feel (Items needed: print the sheets for the week). PLEASE STICK TO THE SCRIPTS AS MUCH AS YOU CAN!

Parent/Caregiver: *Hello everybody! I really like being around this group! Would any of you care for a scrumptious snack (make sure to change it up!)?* (Pause for effect.)

Parent/Caregiver: *Today we are going to talk about why it is important to tell others how you feel.*

Parent/Caregiver: *By communicating with others how we feel, we not only let others know what we are feeling inside, but can effectively start to calm ourselves down. It also opens up lines of communication with others that may be helpful in staying calm in general and especially with our family at home.*

Parent/Caregiver: *This week's mission is to start to use the "I feel" statement This is simply a couple of times per day telling others how we feel, whether that is happy, OK, so-so, sad, mad or otherwise.*

Parent/Caregiver: *Here is a sheet that gives examples of feelings. The main feelings are happy, sad, mad, nervous and embarrassed. However there are many more. Can we think of some additional ones? (make sure they are feelings)*

Parent/Caregiver: *Let's give it a try. How is each one of us feeling right now?*

Parent/Caregiver: *Great job!* (No matter what they said)

Parent/Caregiver: *So every day we will ask each other, "how do we feel?" If we can do this during the week we can earn* _____ (example, making caramel apples or a favorite dessert, or other prize off of the prize bank). *Do we need another brainstorm sheet of prizes to earn?*

I feel _____
because _____

Feeling Options

Happy   Angry   Sad

Shy   Mad

Afraid   Nervous   Worried

Embarrassed   Upset

Disappointed   Hopeful   Silly

Hurt   Excited

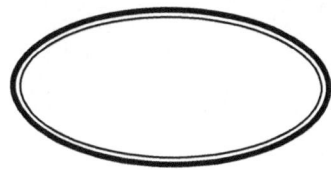   Amazed

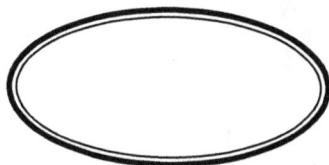   

Help the child translate the because

A child will often say:

"I feel mad because my sister is mean/sucks/made me mad (ex.)"

What they really mean is:

"I feel mad because my sister broke my toy on purpose and she said I was a butthead"

Note: the kid may identify as mad when they really are sad/hurt, they may indicate the wrong reason they are feeling mad. The wrong reason may not be as relatable to others as the real reason. For example, I would be hurt too if someone smashed my toy and called me a butthead.

PARENT ASSIGNMENT

Say, "I understand/I hear you, you feel _____ (example — mad/sad)"

Do not talk them out of it.

Validating how they feel can help them calm down. Later on you can discuss if the level of mad was reasonable.

Setting up clear family rules and consequences, the family agreeing with them, and posting them can having positive impact on the family unit. These predictable rules and consequences provide structure and a sense of calm in knowing what will happen if a rule is broken.

Step 1: Discuss what rules the family should live by. State these rules in a positive manner (leave out the words, "no" and "don't" instead say what we expect. For example, speak nicely to one another, act nicely to one another. Discuss the rules and list them out on a paper to post.

Rules Example:

1. Talk nicely to each other, nice words and nice tone (translated from no yelling).
2. Act nicely to each other, appropriate contact (translated from no hitting).
3. Follow instructions from mom and dad.
4. Eat meals at the table.
5. Go to bed at 8pm.

Step 2: Agree on a set list of consequences. Believe it or not, I have seen kids over and over again set extremely harsh punishments for themselves. So parents should be mindful that the punishment should sort of match the level of the misdeed. However, it should also be something the kid cares about.

One of the important pieces that setting up the consequences with the kids and posting them can do is take the emotion out of the punishment/consequence. For example, a parent could say instead, "oh, too bad for so-and-so that they have to lose their ice cream tonight. Oh, well".

Consequences Example:

1. You get one warning.
2. Then you lose privilege agreed upon such as: no dessert, video game time, TV show, or going somewhere fun.

Step 3: Set up an earning system for following the Family Rules

Following the rules for a set period of time (half days, full days, or hourly) can earn stars or stickers. When a certain number of stickers are reached the kid can choose from the earning bank of prizes agreed upon by the parents/kid. This brings a fun aspect to behaving well and following the rules. It also gives us a leg to stand on when we give the warning/reminder to behave. Go one direction and earn goodies or go the other direction and lose goodies. The choice is yours.

When beginning, it is in everyone's interest to earn something quickly and build buy-in for this plan. It gives something to celebrate and the number of stars needed can increase over time. For example, last week it was 8 stars, next week it is 10 stars to earn a prize. It should also be noted that prizes do not always have to be tangible. Some kids actually prefer to earn family fun night with pizza and movies, alone time with a parent, a trip to a park on the other side of town, ice skating, or going for ice cream.

Directions: Read all ITALICIZED TEXT. Do not read text that is not italicized.

Script for Lesson 12: Family (Items needed: both worksheets for this lesson and a pen/pencil). PLEASE STICK TO THE SCRIPTS AS MUCH AS YOU CAN!

Parent/Caregiver: *Hello, amazing people! Would any of you care for a delectable snack (make sure to change it up!)?* (Pause for effect.)

Parent/Caregiver: *Today we are going to develop together some family rules, or rules of the house. By agreeing on our conduct at home.*

Parent/Caregiver: *We are going to brainstorm what would be good rules for our family to live by. For example, one rule could be that we talk calmly and nicely to one another.*

Parent/Caregiver: *We are going to spend the next few minutes brainstorming ideas for family rules.*

Parent/Caregiver: [Spend 3 minutes brainstorming] *Let's make sure rules are worded positively and highlight behaviors we want to see, rather than the other way around. Which rules did we all agree on?*

Parent/Caregiver: *Next let's brainstorm what the consequences should be for not following the rules. For example, following one warning we might lose a privilege such as TV, electronics, or dessert for that evening.*

Parent/Caregiver: [Spend 3 minutes brainstorming] *What did we decide on for consequences?*

Parent/Caregiver: *Now for the best part: deciding on an award for following the rules. What could we earn as a family if we work on following the rules? Let's brainstorm some ideas.*

Parent/Caregiver: [Spend 3 minutes brainstorming] *What did we decide on? How long will it take for us to earn the reward?*

Parent/Caregiver: *Great job everyone! I know this might not always be an easy assignment, but it could help our family get along better and home could be a calmer place.*

Prize Bank Ideas: Fun family night out or in with great food and activities.

Family Rules and Consequences: Parent Recommendation

Take emotion out of the consequences.

Say, "Oh, too bad for you that you have to lose your _____ "(for example, iPad time)"

(That's it, do not say more. The kid will yell "I don't care" Trust me they care. — Do not engage.)

Brainstorming Family Rules, Consequences, Rewards

Family Rules:

- List them positively

Consequences:

- Set consequences
- Have kids participate

Great Behavior Earns:

Let's choose the best ones to record on our Family Rules and Consequences Agreement Sheet

Family Rules and Consequences Agreement Sheet

Family Rules:

- _____
- _____
- _____
- _____
- _____
- _____
- _____

Consequences: one warning then

- _____
- _____
- _____
- _____

Follow rules? Earn prizes!

Prize bank ideas: _____

_____

_____

_____

_____

_____

How many stickers/stars/smiley faces to earn a prize?

When life gets busy it can be very easy to have a low number of positives during the day. And when a kid is being a pain it is even harder to keep the 10:1 recommended ratio of 10 positives for every constructive feedback (criticism). What is the way to turn this around? The kindness project!

This can be a fun assignment for the week! Easy too, especially if you have to deliberately count the positives said to each other. It can also give us pause to say, "what do I really like about this other person?" I know I love them, but what do I just admire? All kids have hundreds of things to like about them.

Here are some ideas: _____, I want you to know that you are so: _____

(Special, smart, sweet, super, good kid, wonderful, or a great person to hang out with).

During the day say things like, "Great job on _____ "

Also important is extending this kindness to yourself. Tell the kids a couple of things that you like about you. Let them know that it is more than OK to like yourself! It is good to know your strengths! And it is the best example that you can give them of how to have high self-esteem.

You can say, "_____, you know what I really like about me? I am smart and kind too. Guess what? You are those things too, and I am so proud of you — keep it up!

This project could be used for a week in the family, and it could also be used for a week towards others outside of the family. You could have a kindness challenge to do and say 5 kind things per day to others at school, work, or in the community. The family could plan to do something kind for the community like volunteer. Kindness is a positive feeling that spreads goodness to all! Being kind is a great assignment because it is not hard to do! Also, back away from negative people if possible…..it is hard to do the kindness project with them pulling you down. However, if you have a lot of energy one day, these people probably need the kindness project the most.

Directions: Read all ITALICIZED TEXT. Do not read text that is not italicized.

Script for Lesson 13: Family (Items needed: one worksheet and one pen for each family member). PLEASE STICK TO THE SCRIPTS AS MUCH AS YOU CAN!

Parent/Caregiver: *Hello, lovely family! Would any of you care for a good snack (make sure to change it up!)?* (Pause for effect.)

Parent/Caregiver: *Today we are going to do an easier but important lesson: the kindness project.*

Parent/Caregiver: *By the end of the day we can be worn out or stressed, and this can contribute to us not talking as nicely as we should to the people we love the most.*

Parent/Caregiver: *Today is the time to make a plan to move forward with saying kind things to each other during the week.*

Parent/Caregiver: *Let's get out our kindness worksheets and plan to say nice things to each other this week in order to earn a reward!*

Parent Assignment

Say 10 nice things/compliments to each kid daily.

Tally

Kid 1 _____   Kid 2 _____

Keep tally because sometimes it is easy to forget. Check in and encourage each other. Maybe add each other to the list!

Kid Assignment

Assignment: Say 14 nice things to your siblings over the week

Sibling 1 Name: _____   Tally:_____

Sibling 2 Name: _____   Tally:_____

Sibling 3 Name: _____   Tally:_____

Complete this to earn a prize!
What did we decide on? _____

IDEAS FOR NICE THINGS TO SAY:
You are very smart, kind, sweet, creative, fun, talented, or another adjective

I like how you:

I like your:

You are really good at:

How did I do? Did I earn my prize this week?

So, this is an area that I have felt like a hypocrite writing about as of late. However, recently I started lifting some weights and doing push-ups and sit-ups, so I don't feel quite as bad writing about this.

Now that I got that off my chest, research shows that movement in the form of any exercise whatsoever can relieve stress, anxiety, and depression as well as increase focus and calmness. Some people think that hard core exercise is necessary or that they have to be fit — these are fallacies. I could care less if you get any sort of workout in. The trick is the movement. When the brain is stimulated, it helps calm and focus the body, which is very helpful in feeling good.

Similarly, spending time outdoors in green spaces can have a similar affect. Recent studies have shown a significant reduction in stress and anxiety just from hanging out near trees! Seriously!

Movement or spending time outdoors does not even need to be a lengthy commitment. Twenty minutes could be affective and a significant factor in helping everyone in the household feel less stressed from the slog of normal days. School can be stressful. This could be a factor to lifting that stress and in turn could help family members' interactions to be less strained and more positive. For example, after a stressful day people tend to have less patience left and may be close to blowing up just because stress has built up throughout the day.

So what can be done? Some suggestions: take a walk, hike various areas, bike ride, work out, lift weights, do a work out/yoga video, play a sport in the yard with the kids!, visit different gardens/parks, plant some flowers at home, or sit outside with a book.

Directions: Read all ITALICIZED TEXT. Do not read text that is not italicized.

Script for Lesson 14: Family (Items needed: one worksheet for each family member and pens). PLEASE STICK TO THE SCRIPTS AS MUCH AS YOU CAN!

Parent/Caregiver: *Hi and great seeing all of you! Would any of you care for a great snack (make sure to change it up!)? (Pause for effect.)*

Parent/Caregiver: *Today we are going to get each of us moving or outdoors.*

Parent/Caregiver: *Getting our bodies moving or getting outside can lift our spirits and give us more energy over time.*

Parent/Caregiver: *What kinds of things can we each think of that we like to do that involves getting our bodies moving or being outdoors for a bit? Let's get out our planning sheets.*

Parent/Caregiver: *Our goal is to get moving or be outdoors for 20 minutes per day. Let's meet our goal for the week and earn something new!*

The Plan: Get Moving and/or Get Outdoors!

What could we get on the calendar?

Examples: walking, soccer, football, basketball, playing with the dog, biking, hiking, visiting parks, reading outside, playing outside, weights, jumping jack, etc.

Did I get moving or get outside for 20 minutes?

MONDAY	TUESDAY	WEDNESDAY	THURSDAY	FRIDAY	SATURDAY	SUNDAY

Way to go! Earn a trip to Laser Tag (example)!

Ideas to earn: _____

Being aware of how our bodies feel can greatly help with being able to focus and stay calm. Throughout our days stress and anxiety will naturally build up in each one of us. One way to release some of those unwanted feelings is to take 5 minutes per day to complete a quiet breathing or mindfulness task.

This is a great mission for the entire family to try out because research shows that breathing and mindfulness can lower anxiety and stress for all ages! It also gives everyone a nice, 5 minute break from each other and time to reset and center ourselves.

I used to think that these exercises were a load of hooey. But through the overwhelming research as well as viewing so much success with clients, I have come to realize that this can be a very powerful tool with little time and effort. Also, in my office I tend to use this exercise to help people, and I teach them what to do. I can absolutely tell the difference in myself before and after the task.

Once breathing has been mastered over the course of weeks, this newly acquired skill can be used almost anywhere. However, breathing is a skill that takes practice, sort of like a sport. You would not go in to play in the championship game without practice — same goes for breathing. The exercise on the next page should be done for 4 weeks when the person is calm (not when the person is mad/upset). That way they can master the breathing and a month from now he or she can start using this strategy when they realize they are becoming upset.

LESSON 15.1: Breathing and Mindfulness

Directions: Read all ITALICIZED TEXT. Do not read text that is not italicized.

Script for Lesson 15: Family (Items needed: one worksheet for each family member and pens). PLEASE STICK TO THE SCRIPTS AS MUCH AS YOU CAN!

Parent/Caregiver: *Hi beautiful people! Would any of you care for a lovely snack (make sure to change it up!)? (Pause for effect.)*

Parent/Caregiver: *Today we are going to do talk about breathing and mindfulness.*

Parent/Caregiver: *Taking 5 minutes to sit quietly, breathe slowly, and clear your mind can bring a calm feeling to the body and mind.*

Parent/Caregiver: *This is an easy week for us! The assignment is only 5 minutes per day and we each do the breathing in our own rooms when we are feeling calm.*

Parent/Caregiver: *Let's give the exercise on the handouts a try. Everyone find a place to get comfy (maybe the living room?) We get comfy, take a breath in and hold for 5 seconds (about) then breathe out VERY VERY VERY SLOWLY. This part of breathing out slowly is what makes this exercise work and it takes practice.*

Parent/Caregiver: *This is a great one for us this week! Easy peasy in that we practice this on our own for 5 minutes each day and earn a prize! Let's do it.*

Directions: Lay in a comfy chair or bed completely loose (arms and legs on the chair or bed). Breathe in and hold for 5 seconds, then breathe out very, very slowly (5 seconds). This should be done when the person is calm for the first few weeks. It can easily be completed right before going to sleep because this is a calming exercise.

	MONDAY	TUESDAY	WEDNESDAY	THURSDAY	FRIDAY	SATURDAY	SUNDAY
Practice Breathing 5 times per day							
How did I feel afterwards?							

LESSON 16.0: Basic Behavior Plan

This is hands down the lesson that I facilitate most often in my office. Parents come in saying here is the problem behavior and we need that behavior to change. Most often times the child or teenager would also like this series of behaviors and unfortunate events to also change. It is really no fun for anyone.

The keys to success of a behavior plan are as follows:

1. Only one behavior can be worked on at a time. So if a child is hitting others and also yelling, we can only effectively work on the hitting first. After that behavior is tackled, then we can move to work on the yelling.

2. The child needs to be a part of putting the behavior plan together. He or she needs to be a part of choosing the reward and the consequence. This will increase buy in from the kiddo and increase the chances of this plan working.

3. Tracking the amount of behaviors is important to understanding if the plan is working. Most likely a behavior will not completely stop right away, but will be greatly reduced (which is a success). However, it is human nature to be perturbed if the behavior continues even at all so it is important to realize if the hitting behavior has gone from 10 times per week down to 3 times per week. It is not perfect yet, but it is going in the right direction.

4. Behavior plans are only effective temporarily. They are mainly effective in grabbing a child's attention and helping them on a short term basis. Should a behavior plan be in place longer, then it would need to be constantly updated with new expectations and novel rewards. It is not meant to be a long-term solution.

5. If a mistake is made the responses should be "oh darn, I guess we'll have to try better next time." We all have bad days sometimes.

Directions: Read all ITALICIZED TEXT. Do not read text that is not italicized.

Script for Lesson 16: Family (Items needed: one worksheet for each family member and pens). PLEASE STICK TO THE SCRIPTS AS MUCH AS YOU CAN!

Parent/Caregiver: *Hi wonderful family! Would any of you care for a delicious snack* (make sure to change it up!)*?* (Pause for effect.)

Parent/Caregiver: *Today we are going to make a plan to improve one behavior for each of us. Everyone can each work on something to improve including parents!*

Parent/Caregiver: *For example, my goal is going to be to change the behavior of _____. I think that meeting this goal will make me feel _____ because _____.*

Parent/Caregiver: *When we improve our behaviors we end up feeling more calm at home.*

Parent/Caregiver: *Let's take a minute to think with our parents about what one behavior we could work on this week. What would be the most helpful for me to work on? What would be the most helpful to my family? We all have to work on one, but we do get to earn a prize!*

Parent/Caregiver: *We have to remember we can't be perfect but working on improving behaviors can help us feel better at home!* (Parents too!)

Example Behavior Plan

Behaviors wanted: Listening to mom. Following directions. Saying nice things.

	MONDAY	TUESDAY	WEDNESDAY	THURSDAY	FRIDAY	SATURDAY	SUNDAY
Morning							
Afternoon							
Evening							
Bedtime							

Reward: Every time I do a great job I put a smiley or star. 10 smileys = Ice cream.

Consequence: After 1 warning, I lose a privilege such as video game time.

Behavior Plan

Behaviors wanted:

	MONDAY	TUESDAY	WEDNESDAY	THURSDAY	FRIDAY	SATURDAY	SUNDAY
Morning							
Afternoon							
Evening							
Bedtime							

Reward: Every time I do a great job I _____. # _____ earns the reward of _____

Consequence: After 1 warning, lose a privilege such as _____

_____

Unfortunately, screentime (meaning use of computers, television, iPads, video games or cell phones) very likely contributes to moodiness, irritability, anger, feeling down, and sleep disturbance (meaning people are having a harder time falling asleep). Recent research also suggests that there is an addictive quality to screens. I myself can give my own example in that I often times watch Netflix on my phone with earbuds while waiting for my toddler to settle down and fall asleep. It is easy to lose track of time and watch more episodes than originally intended. It is not uncommon for teenagers to lose track of time completely and then watch or play something on electronics far into the night. This can contribute to many difficulties during the week including moodiness and being tired.

The task assigned this week will probably be a challenging one for families. However, that in itself is telling in how reliant we really are on electronics. In addition, our brain chemistry is likely changing based on technology and computers.

My popularity goes right down the tubes when I suggest that kids between 8 and 12 give up Minecraft for the weekdays. However, I have observed incredible results when the "weekend only" model is followed, meaning that without the electronics I observed happier, more well-rested kiddos who are not as moody. Typically I encourage families to let kids earn electronic time during the week that can be "cashed in" on the weekend. However, if the kiddo cannot stay in a pleasant demeanor on the weekend then I can go even further and recommend that there is just a moratorium or hiatus for electronics until further notice. This has been recommended only in severe circumstances.

An easy way to naturally make this transition is to have kids placed in sports or activities after school. Many people have indicated their concerns about the kid being too overextended and it impacting grades. However, the research on sports and activities is exactly the opposite. Those in sports actually attain higher grades for a variety of reasons. Anyway, the more time on those activities, the less time for boredom and electronics.

Directions: Read all ITALICIZED TEXT. Do not read text that is not italicized.

Script for Lesson 17: Family (Items needed: one worksheet for each family member and pens). PLEASE STICK TO THE SCRIPTS AS MUCH AS YOU CAN! This assignment will probably not be the most popular, but it could be the most strikingly beneficial. We will need to break out the big prizes for this week for all involved, and we may have to shorten the goal to just the 5 day school week.

Parent/Caregiver: *Hello family I adore! Would any of you care for a special snack* (make sure to change it up!)*?* (Pause for effect.)

Parent/Caregiver: *Today we are going to talk about dum dum dum…..electronics.*

Parent/Caregiver: *Unfortunately the new research on electronics is not so good. Screentime has now been linked to addiction, moodiness, irritability, and even brain changes associated with trouble paying attention.*

Parent/Caregiver: *So this week is the Zero Electronics Challenge for the household.* (Pause for the groans.)

Parent/Caregiver: *I know this idea is not too popular, but that's why we are going to up the ante with the prize for the week. Let's pick a better prize and try it this week. Believe it or not the school week is usually really busy and we might not even miss it too much!*

Parent/Caregiver: *Let's try it and see if we notice any differences in our household. Ready? Go!*

Reward for Zero Electronic Challenge

What can we do instead?

- Books (new book)
- Activity (sport, 4H, church club, Lego club, Robots, Dance, Theater)
- Get outside (trails, biking, snow shoeing, skiing)
- Music is still OK!
- Reward for zero electronics/week (something good)
  = _____ ?

What happened as a result?

_____

_____

_____

_____

_____

_____

An area that I think is highly worth mentioning is the sensory factor that seems to wreak havoc on many families because there are some members sensitive to certain input. Do you have any members that seem to be extra sensitive to tags on clothes, crowds, repetitive noises, loud sounds, certain people talking, smells, foods, touch, or pain? Turns out these sensitive souls are likely not making it up. The world is now discovering that we don't all feel sensory input in the same way — so if two people cut their foot on a rock and one says it hurts really, really, really bad, and the other person says it doesn't even hurt they both are likely telling the truth. The one that is more sensitive is at a higher risk for getting upset due to sensory input. For example, does the sensitive member of the family seem to melt down for "no reason?"

Some people are very sensitive to noises that are loud or repetitive. To them, these noises are like nails on a chalkboard. The sound is horrible and causes them distress. Recently, I was trying to focus at an office where there was a constant "pinging" noise. Ping! Ping! Ping! Ping! I looked around and somehow no one else seemed to be bothered by this, but I found it incredibly difficult for me to concentrate. The pinging and interruption of my thinking contributed to me becoming annoyed and agitated even. However the noise did not appear to do this to others.

Why am I mentioning this? We each have things we are sensitive to that may contribute to becoming irritable as well as interfering with our attention. If we could remove these "sensory agitators" or deal with them more effectively, the home environment would likely become more peaceful.

LESSON 18.1: Sensory Survival

Directions: Read all ITALICIZED TEXT. Do not read text that is not italicized.

Script for Lesson 18: Family (Items needed: one worksheet for each family member and pens). PLEASE STICK TO THE SCRIPTS AS MUCH AS YOU CAN! Whew, an easy one this week!

Parent/Caregiver: *Hello all! Would any of you care for a yummy snack (make sure to change it up!)? (Pause for effect.)*

Parent/Caregiver: *Today we are going to do talk about sensory factors in our daily lives that can impact us.*

Parent/Caregiver: *Sensory includes: sound, sight, taste, smell, and how our bodies feel in the space around it.*

Parent/Caregiver: *For example, some people have a hard time with loud or repetitive noises, crowded places, or things like tags in their shirts.*

Parent/Caregiver: *Those with severe sensory problems describe even small sounds as being like nails on a chalkboard. I myself am a little sensitive to: _____.*

Parent/Caregiver: *The goal of this week is to start to notice if we each are sensitive to any sensory input around us and start to figure out how to help with this. If we aren't able to think of anything specific, this might mean adding back in our quiet break of ten minutes in a quiet, calm, clean area by ourselves. What could taking this type of a break do for our sensory systems? That's right, it can calm each of our sensory systems down.*

Parent/Caregiver: *Let's get out our sheets and start thinking about the sensory world around us!*

Sensory Sensitivities

Do smells bother me? → Take a satchel of things to smell

Do crowds bother me? → Shop during off hours → Go to events early or use off-peak hours to avoid crowds

Do noises bother me? → Buy earbuds or headphones specifically in the car → Buy noise canceling or sound machine → Take quiet breaks

Does touch bother me? → Let people know to ask you before they hug or touch you.

Do tags bother me? → Take all the tags out. Buy tag-less shirt.

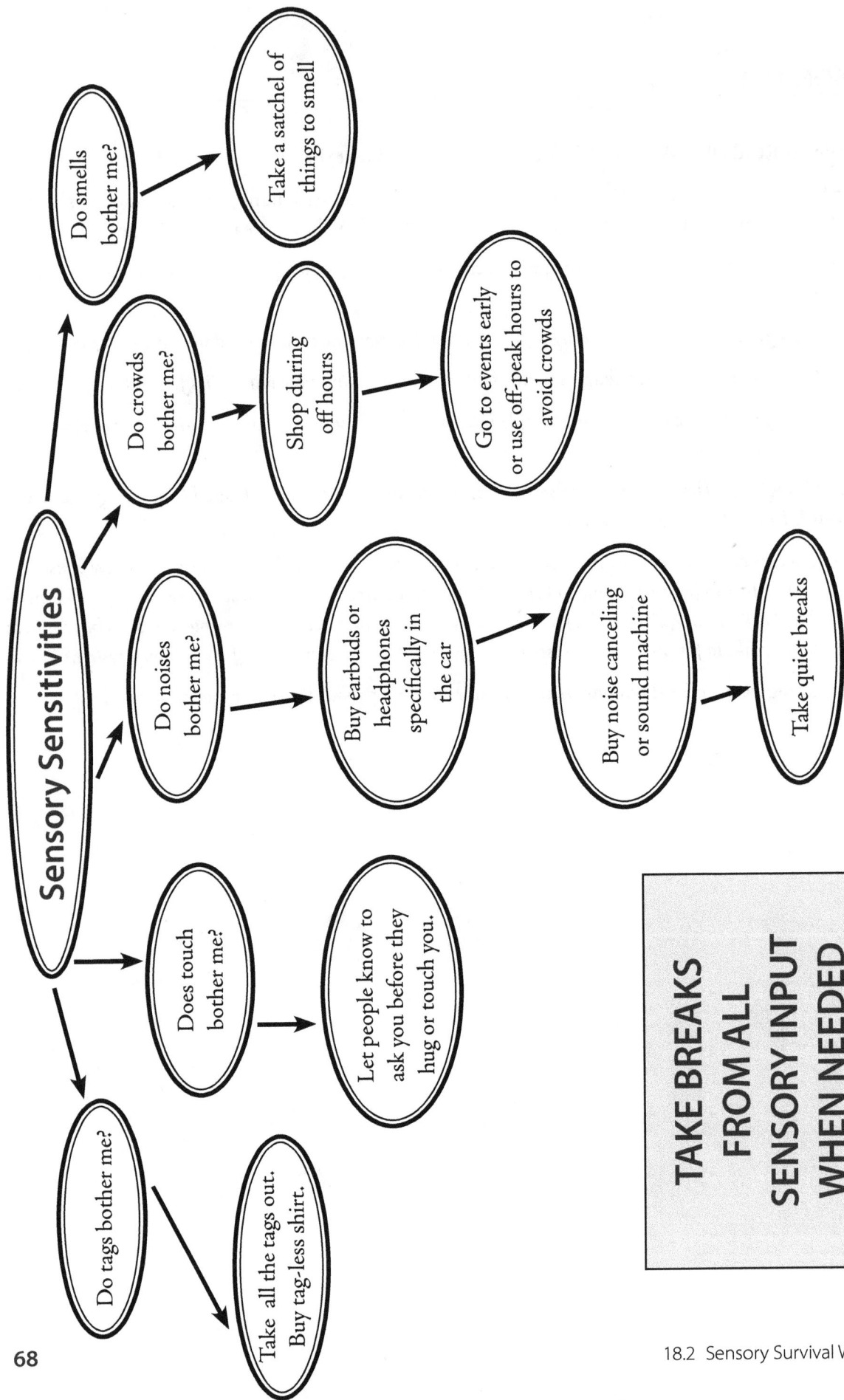

TAKE BREAKS FROM ALL SENSORY INPUT WHEN NEEDED

18.2 Sensory Survival Worksheet 1

Sensory Survival Brainstorm

Name: _____

What in the sensory world is a little irritating to me?

Too much noise? _____

Too loud of noise?_____

People being too close?_____

White artificial lights?_____

Crowds?_____

Tags in clothes?_____

Other factors:_____

_____

_____

What can I try to help minimize this irritation?

More quiet breaks

Use of headphones in the car

Cutting out tags

Being in crowds

Other:_____

_____

_____

_____

If none identified then resume a quiet break for the week preferably right after school or work. This should be a 10-minute break without electronics. It should be in a completely quiet, calm, clean zone by yourself.

Reducing Sensory Agitators for the Week

Name: _____

What's my plan to reduce sensory agitators this week?

_____

_____

_____

Days of the week (fill in the names)							
Did I do the plan?							
How did I feel today? Did I notice anything?							

LESSON 19.0: Something Good First

This assignment seeks to lift the spirits and the morale by fighting the human nature, which is to focus on the negative and lead with the negative when thinking and communicating with others. We need to fight this urge! It is very important for children to see that they need to lead with the positive. Yes, we all have a VERY bad day from time to time where there is not much good to mention. However, for the most part there is typically something positive to mention about a trip, experiences, your day, and other events. The trick is that if a day went 99% good, the 1% bad is what stands out in your mind. However, if you lead with the 1% bad, the mind starts to follow making experiences remembered and feelings more negative.

The answer? Force yourself to "Lead with the Good." The Lead with the Good Challenge challenges family members to give three positives before reporting a negative. This can be quite tricky because it tends to be a habit to announce the bad thing that happened to a group of people. So what can we do? Make this a fun challenge! All involved can earn a prize at the end of the week for reporting 3 good things from the day (school or work or whatever). Unfortunately the family members will also get zinged if they lead with the negative. For example, the group should agree on a funny word or sound to say if a member forgets the "Lead with the Positive" theme of the week. They can say the word, "zing" in a funny voice to alert of the mistake. Or the group could go farther and bean each other with a marshmallow or something that would make things fun.

Leading with the positive is a habit that, over time, can lead to a more positive based attitude for the entire family. Sometimes it is easy to forget in this rushed and stressful world: why are we taking life this seriously? Shouldn't it be more fun and contain more laughter? Can't we make a tiny amount of time for enjoying our family members who we love more than anything in this world?

Directions: Read all ITALICIZED TEXT. Do not read text that is not italicized.

Script for Lesson 19: Family (Items needed: one worksheet and pens). PLEASE STICK TO THE SCRIPTS AS MUCH AS YOU CAN!

Parent/Caregiver: *Hello lovely group! Would any of you like a munchie* (make sure to change it up!)? (Pause for effect.)

Parent/Caregiver: *Today we are going to talk about this week's lesson entitled, "Something Good First."*

Parent/Caregiver: *Unfortunately even if most of our day has gone well, the thing that will stick out most in the human mind is the one negative event.*

Parent/Caregiver: *When we talk about the negative occurrence first, this will tend to lead to feeling worse.*

Parent/Caregiver: *So we are going to do the challenge to say three good things first (and at least three good things every day).*

Parent/Caregiver: *This lesson can be challenging for certain minds, so we will have a decent prize this week if we can manage it. We will also have to figure out what to do if someone forgets and says the negative first. We could get to be silly and say "zing!"*

Parent/Caregiver: *We all get one free pass just in case one of us has a really bad day. Then it is OK to fore go the assignment (just for that day).*

Parent/Caregiver: *So let's all get started on saying something good first!!!*

THE CHALLENGE
SOMETHING GOOD FIRST!

When reporting on our day or an event we *all* say 3 positives *before* reporting the negative!

Names of
Family
Members

	MONDAY	TUESDAY	WEDNESDAY	THURSDAY	FRIDAY	SATURDAY	SUNDAY
1.							
2.							
3.							
4.							
5.							
6.							

Easy way to practice...how was our day?

Did we do it and report positive first?

Great! What should we earn this week?_____

Prize Idea: Earn a trip to the bookstore. Everyone earns a book!

What will we do for fun if someone fore?_____

For example, we could say, "Zing!"

One thing I would be remiss not to mention in a book looking to improve family functioning is to make sure all family members are getting their basic needs met. For example, if we are not rested then all heck can break loose at home and can disrupt the family unit. In fact, after school and in the evening we are tired after a long day and the lack of enough sleep and food can cause some serious moodiness and irritability. Eating, sleeping, self-care, and feeling loved are all basic necessary components of life, without which humans cannot function or excel.

The American style of life is very busy. The busier we get the more likely it is that some of our basic needs will go by the wayside. Having basic needs unmet makes the rest of life functioning significantly harder.

Are members getting enough to eat? Do any of them run out of gas during the afternoon? Can we solve this by carrying some portable snacks with us or in the car? What can we do to reduce "hangry" times during the day and night. A lack of sleep, food, (shelter and safety as well), and a sense of belonging and support will typically lead to, among other things, feeling grumpy. As we all know, a grumpy family member can wreak havoc on family interactions and can (temporarily) wreck a peaceful home ambiance that we are trying to foster.

LESSON 20.1: Basic Needs

Directions: Read all ITALICIZED TEXT. Do not read text that is not italicized.

Script for Lesson 20: Family (Items needed: two worksheets and a pen for each family member). PLEASE STICK TO THE SCRIPTS AS MUCH AS YOU CAN!

Parent/Caregiver: *Hello one and all! You get more good looking every day! Would any of you like a scrumdiddlyumptious snackeroo* (make sure to change it up!)? (Pause for effect.)

Parent/Caregiver: *Today we are going to talk about making sure we have all of our basic needs met.*

Parent/Caregiver: *Basic needs include making sure we have enough to eat and sleep. It also includes taking care of ourselves both physically and emotionally. It is also important to have a sense of belonging and feel that we have a support system around us.*

Parent/Caregiver: *If these components of basic needs are not met, functioning in other areas of life such as school or work can become much more difficult.*

Parent/Caregiver: *This week we are each going to assess our basic needs in order to identify where we can improve them.*

Parent/Caregiver: *By taking better care of ourselves, we will feel better and do better both at home and at school or work.*

Parent/Caregiver: *So let's all get started on assessing our basic needs!!!*

Basic Needs Brainstorm

Name: _____

How much sleep am I getting?

Hours _____   Hours needed _____

Plan to increase sleep_____

Am I getting enough to eat? Are there times of the day when I feel too hungry?

Eating enough?_____   Times of the day when I am over hungry?_____

Am I eating anything healthy? _____

Plan to improve eating _____

Am I taking care of myself?

Am I showered/bathed?_____   Am I groomed (teeth, hair, nails)?_____

Plan to improve self-care_____

Am I getting at least a tiny break in my day?

Do I have at least one 10-minute break?_____

Plan to add one break _____

Do I have one thing I actually like doing on my calendar this week?

Is there something on my schedule this week I enjoy?_____

Plan to add an enjoyable event one per week_____

Do I have one person I can talk to at home if I have a rotten day?

Is there someone I feel I can confide in who will support me?_____

Make a plan to check in with a parent during the week and put it on the calendar _____

Improving Basic Needs

Name: _____

What's my plan to improve on basic needs this week? Be specific.

_____

_____

_____

	MONDAY	TUESDAY	WEDNESDAY	THURSDAY	FRIDAY	SATURDAY	SUNDAY
Did I do the plan?							
How did I feel by the end of the week? Did I notice anything?							

PARENT CHAPTERS

LESSON 21: It is OK to take a day off (unplanned, unapproved) two days per year

One of the best pieces of advice I have received from one of my mentors was that it was "OK" for me to "take a Mental Health day or two" each calendar year. I was surprised to hear a supervisor say this to me. She was not saying, if you are deathly ill or have a seriously contagious condition, call in. No — she was saying that if mentally I was exhausted, it was OK — no encouraged to take a day away.

I have contemplated over the years the wisdom of this statement. My family has classically had a very opposite approach to school and work. For example, if my arm was falling off, I am pretty sure that my parents would have hauled me into school citing that I did not have a fever and I was going.

But as I have worked with more and more kids over the years, I have come to agree with my supervisor. Consider the following example: a kid has a VERY rough morning. Then has a rough gym class in which he gets knocked around by another student, he then gets back to his regular classroom and someone calls him a name. He blows up and strikes a girl in the face. He is expelled for this action and the school police officer even gets involved for possible legal action. Now — hind sight is 20/20. If given the choice between out of school suspension for a week vs one day off....it seems that I would choose one day off in order to not have a suspension on a child's record. What's more, even though we can't really predict the future, there might really have been some warning signs that things could go terribly wrong.

Sometimes in life regrouping is what I would suggest. But no more than 2 days per year. And you don't have to share this with the child (as in come up with some other reason you kept them home — like we have an appointment scheduled ....that somehow got canceled right before).

Note: This assignment is best done with a partner who can keep you on track because this can be difficult to do.

Yes, we need limits. Kids cannot have everything. However, for some kids (and adults too) the word, "no" triggers anger. Personally, for me the word, "relax" triggers anger. Do not tell me to relax. DO NOT TELL ME TO RELAX.

So how else could you say "no?"

Here are some options:

Not right now, but we can plan to _____.

Maybe later/tomorrow/next week.

Well we can't today unfortunately because of _____ but let's plan on next week/some other time.

Redirect attention to something else.

Take the time to plan out when you can do the preferred activity. Try to understand the child's feelings. Yes, I wish we could go swimming too! There just is not enough time today for that, but I would love to go tomorrow. And if we can do really well at the _____, maybe we can _____ (something semi fun).

Why does this help? Some of us get triggered by certain words and it does not matter what it is — if the certain word is spoken they are going to be mad. That happens for a lot of kids who are told no a lot.

I included a pre and post evaluation for families to use to generate a list of goals and quantify those goals. That way by half way through the lessons you should be able to see that it is working for your family (or not and make adjustments).

In addition to the pre and post evaluation, please generate three family goals using positive language and quantifiable markers so that you can measure progress. For example I would like you to use the pretest to help generate ideas for goals and then come up with two or three main goals for your family during this program.

Examples of goals:

1. Family members will talk nicely to one another using a calm, normal tone of voice (aka less yelling).

2. Family members will say nice things to one another, positive things and compliments (aka less rips, tear-downs, and taunting).

3. Create and maintain a calmer and happier home environment — family members work together to keep the house neat, organized, and calmer (less mess, clutter, disorganization).

Each of the above examples could be measured through the provided Pre and Post Test on the following page. However if your family's goal cannot be measured by the provided tool then you can create your own on the following worksheet.

Then measure the using the same indicator following the use of the lessons. Keep in mind that goals should be realistic. Teenagers tend to be snotty and snarky. It will be a failing goal if the goal is for your teen to talk nicely 100% of the time because often times they don't even know what they sound like.

Please go to *www.hurdpsychology.com* to share your pre and post/family goals results.

How often do we say nice things to one another?

       Never (1)   Some (2)   A lot (3)   Always (4)

How often do we talk nicely to one another using a nice tone of voice?

       Never (1)   Some (2)   A lot (3)   Always (4)

What is our level of happiness at home?

       None (1)   A Little (2)   Some (3)   A Lot (4)

What is our level of calm at home?

       None (1)   A Little (2)   Some (3)   A Lot (4)

How often are our feelings towards one another positive?

       Never (1)   Some (2)   A lot (3)   Always (4)

Date of Pre-Evaluation: _____

Total Score (add all circled scores): _____

How Many Lessons Did We Complete: _____

Date of Post-Evaluation: _____

Total Score (add all circled scores): _____

Please go to *www.hurdpsychology.com* to share your pre and post results.

Family Goals Worksheet

Directions: Please phrase three family goals positively. Complete this page before and after the completion of the lessons. This can be used with the Pre and Post Evaluation.

What is the goal? _____

How often does this currently occur?

      Never (1)   Some (2)   A lot (3)   Always (4)

What is the goal? _____

How often does this currently occur?

      Never (1)   Some (2)   A lot (3)   Always (4)

What is the goal? _____

How often does this currently occur?

      Never (1)   Some (2)   A lot (3)   Always (4)

Date of Pre-Evaluation: _____

Total Score (add all circled scores): _____

How Many Lessons Did We Complete: _____

Date of Post-Evaluation: _____

Total Score (add all circled scores): _____

Please go to *www.hurdpsychology.com* to share your family goals pre and post results.

www.ingramcontent.com/pod-product-compliance
Lightning Source LLC
Chambersburg PA
CBHW081151040426
42445CB00015B/1832